PETS' GUIDES

Slinky's Guide to

Caring for Your Snake

Isabel Thomas

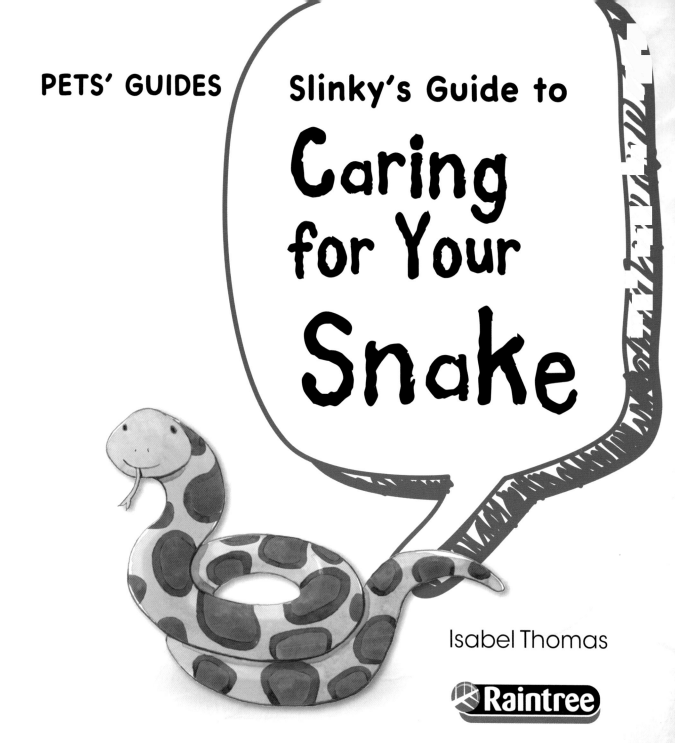

Raintree

Raintree is an imprint of Capstone Global Library Limited, a company incorporated in England and Wales having its registered office at 7 Pilgrim Street, London, EC4V 6LB – Registered company number: 6695582

www.raintreepublishers.co.uk
myorders@raintreepublishers.co.uk

Edited by James Benefield and Brynn Baker
Designed by Cynthia Akiyoshi
Picture research by Tracy Cummins
Production by Victoria Fitzgerald
Originated by Capstone Global Library Limited
Printed and bound in China by RR Donnelley Asia
ISBN 978-1-406-28179-8

18 17 16 15 14
10 9 8 7 6 5 4 3 2 1

British Library Cataloguing in Publication Data
A full catalogue record for this book is available from the British Library.

Acknowledgements
We would like to thank the following for permission to reproduce photographs: Alamy: © Juniors Bildarchiv GmbH, 13, 14, © ZUMA Press, Inc., 7; Capstone Library: Karon Dubke, 5, 11, 20, 25, 26; Getty Images: John Cancalosi, 18, Russell Illig, 8; Shutterstock: Joel Kempson, 16, Willie Davis, front cover; Superstock: imagebroker.net, 23; Design Elements Shutterstock: iBird, Picsfive, R-studio.

We would like to thank Alan H. Wilkie for his assistance in the preparation of this book.

Every effort has been made to contact copyright holders of material reproduced in this book. Any omissions will be rectified in subsequent printings if notice is given to the publisher.

All the Internet addresses (URLs) given in this book were valid at the time of going to press. However, due to the dynamic nature of the Internet, some addresses may have changed, or sites may have changed or ceased to exist since publication. While the author and publisher regret any inconvenience this may cause readers, no responsibility for any such changes can be accepted by either the author or the publisher.

Contents

Some words are shown in bold, **like this**. You can find out what they mean by looking in the glossary.

Do you want a pet snake?

Howdy! I'm Slinky and this book is about pet snakes like me. Did you know that some snakes make great pets? It's amazing to watch us and learn how we live.

Snakes are **reptiles**, and we need special care. Before getting a pet snake, be sure you can look after me properly. I'll need a safe, clean place to live, the right kind of food, places to hide and explore, and **vet** care if I get sick or injured.

Choosing your snake

You will need expert help to choose a snake. Corn snakes like me are some of the most common pet snakes. We have beautiful colours and patterns. Milk snakes, rat snakes and king snakes are often kept as pets, too. Ask the expert if I'm supposed to feel smooth or rough. This will help you know if I'm ill.

Some snakes are too big to be kept as pets. Look at this python! It is kept in special conditions, in a zoo!

Find out how long I will live and how big I will get. Make sure that you will be able to give me enough space as I grow. Some snakes grow much too big to be kept as pets.

I am happy to be kept as a pet because I was born in **captivity**. Never buy a snake that has been taken from the wild. The best places to get a pet snake are good **breeders**, **animal shelters** and **rescue centres**.

A healthy snake has bright eyes, smooth skin and a flicking tongue. Ask to see its feeding and **shedding** record, too. This is where an owner writes down how well a snake eats and sheds its skin.

Getting ready

Your snake will live in a special tank called a **vivarium**. Ask a vet or an expert that knows all about snakes to help you choose the right type. My vivarium will need to be at least as long as me, so I can stretch out. Remember, I will need more space as I grow!

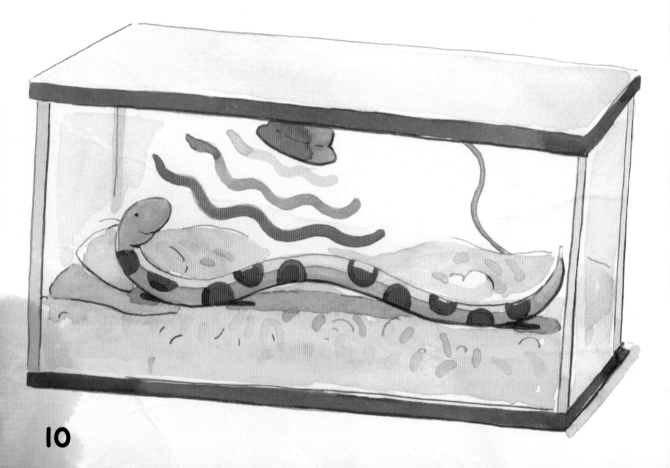

The temperature and **humidity** inside the vivarium must be right. They should match your snake's wild **habitat**. Set up my home at least a week before I move in. Check the temperature and humidity often. If it's too hot, I can die! You can use a **thermostat**.

Don't forget the furniture! I will need:

- Rough rocks to help me shed my skin.
- Hiding places at the warm and cool ends of my vivarium.
- Branches for climbing. Buy specially cleaned branches from a pet shop.

Snakes spend lots of time **basking** in the heat and cooling off in the shade, but we like exploring, too. Change my furniture every so often so I don't get bored. You could make new hiding places out of cardboard tubes, boxes or plant pots.

Welcome home

When my vivarium is ready, it's time to bring me home. Small snakes can be carried in a plastic box with a lid. Make sure the box has air holes and doesn't get too warm or too cool. Larger snakes need a cotton bag tied tightly at the top.

Find out how many hours of light and darkness your snake needs. Corn snakes like me like it to be light when the sun is up and dark when the sun goes down. Snakes are very good at escaping. Attach the vivarium lid tightly, and make sure there are no holes.

Feeding time

Most pet snakes eat **rodents**, such as mice or small rats. Pet shops sell frozen rodents that are just the right size for my mouth. I can swallow a meal one and a half times the size of my head. Gulp!

Snakes don't need breakfast, lunch and dinner. Most grown-up snakes only need one meal a week. Feed me outside my vivarium, so I don't eat my bedding by mistake. I also need clean drinking water in a heavy bowl so it won't tip over.

Shedding

Snakes shed their scaly skin as they grow. You can watch me do this several times a year. My skin goes dull and I move around less. My eyes look cloudy and I may not want to eat. Please don't touch me while I'm shedding.

Give me a large water bowl to soak in, and
make sure I have rocks to rub my head on.
When I've finished shedding, take the old
skin away. Gently remove any old skin left
on my body.

Handling

Snakes can be shy, and we don't like to be handled very often. Try not to pick me up more than three or four times a week.

- Wash your hands before and after you handle me.

- Move slowly and be gentle.

- Support my whole body using both hands.

- Hold me loosely so I can move through your hands without getting hurt.

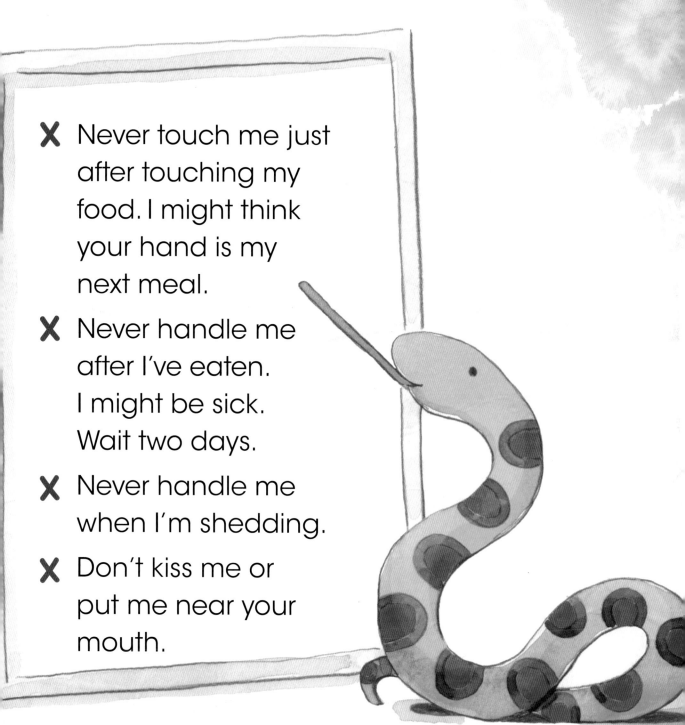

X Never touch me just after touching my food. I might think your hand is my next meal.

X Never handle me after I've eaten. I might be sick. Wait two days.

X Never handle me when I'm shedding.

X Don't kiss me or put me near your mouth.

Keeping me healthy

Write down when I eat and shed my skin. You could record my weight and length, too. A healthy snake eats, sheds and grows well. If you spot any signs of sickness, take me to visit a vet who knows a lot about snakes.

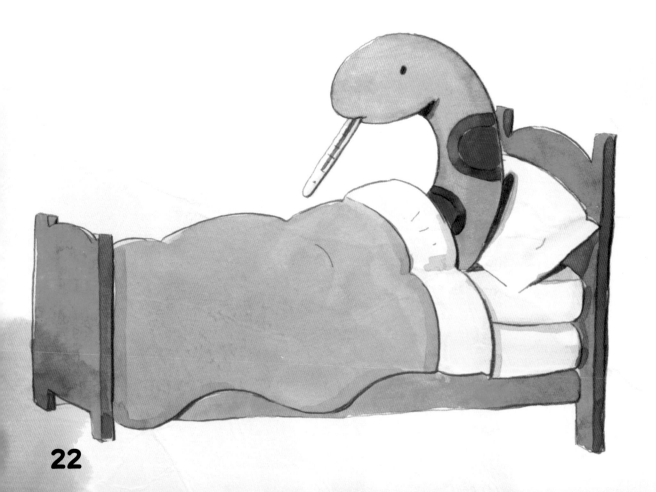

Slinky's Health Check:

- Check my tongue. Is it flicking in and out quickly, tasting the air? The ends should not be stuck together.

- Check my body. Does it feel firm?

- Check my skin. It should not have any blisters or lumps. Can you see any **mites**?

- Check my nostrils. Do I have a runny nose? Am I having trouble breathing?

Cleaning my home

Snakes need clean homes to stay healthy, so check my vivarium every day. Make sure the temperature and humidity are just right. Take away any damp or dirty bedding. Change the water in my water bowl, especially if I've taken a bath in it.

You will need to clean the whole vivarium about once a month. While you're cleaning, keep me in my travelling box or bag. Use special cleaning products that are safe for reptiles. Rinse everything and make sure it is completely dry before you put me back in.

Help from other people

If you would like to keep a pet snake, you will need help from other people. Ask experts to help you choose the right snake. Find a vet nearby who knows about caring for snakes. You will also need a grown-up to help you care for your snake at home.

When you go on holiday, teach someone
else how to look after me while you are away.
They will need to visit every day to keep my
vivarium clean and check that I'm happy
and healthy. Don't forget to send me a
postcard!

Snake facts

- There are nearly 3,000 different types of snakes. Not all snakes make good pets.

- Most snakes eat meat. Some eat fish, insects and bird eggs. Before you get a pet snake, find out what it eats.

- Most snakes like to live on their own, but some can be kept in small groups.

- Anacondas are the world's largest snakes. They can grow up to 10 metres (33 feet) long. They do not make good pets.

Slinky's top tips

Watch me carefully if I'm sick after eating. I may be unwell or unhappy.

- Ask a vet or reptile expert to help you choose a pet snake, find a good breeder and learn how to care for your new pet.

- Never touch snakes that you spot in the wild. They could be dangerous.

If you already have pet snakes, **quarantine** your new pet to make sure it doesn't have an illness it could pass on to the others.

Glossary

animal shelter organization that cares for animals that do not have homes

basking lying in a warm or bright place

breeder person who helps animals have babies in an organized way

captivity kept by humans instead of living in the wild

habitat natural home of a wild animal

humidity how much water vapour there is in the air

mite tiny spider-like bugs that lives on larger animals

quarantine keeping a new pet away from other animals to make sure it does not pass on an illness

reptile type of animal with scaly skin that usually lays eggs with soft shells

rescue centre organization that rescues animals that are lost, injured or not being taken care of properly

rodent type of animal with front teeth that never stop growing, such as mice and rats

shedding losing the top layer of old skin

thermostat device that controls how hot or cold it is in a room or an enclosure, such as a vivarium

vet person trained to care for ill or injured animals

vivarium special home for a pet where the temperature and other conditions can be made to match what it would be like in the wild

Find out more

Books

If You Were a Snake, Clare Hibbert
   (Franklin Watts, 2013)

Pets Plus: Lizards and Snakes, Sally Morgan
   (Franklin Watts, 2011)

Snake (The Pet to Get), Rob Colson (Wayland 2014)

Websites

www.rspca.org.uk/allaboutanimals/pets/other
The website of the RSPCA (Royal Society for the Prevention of Cruelty to Animals) has important advice and factsheets if you are thinking about caring for a pet snake. There are factsheets about corn snakes, common rat snakes, royal or ball pythons and common garter snakes.

Index